WRITER'S TOOLBOX

Art Panels, BAM! Speech Bubbles, POW!

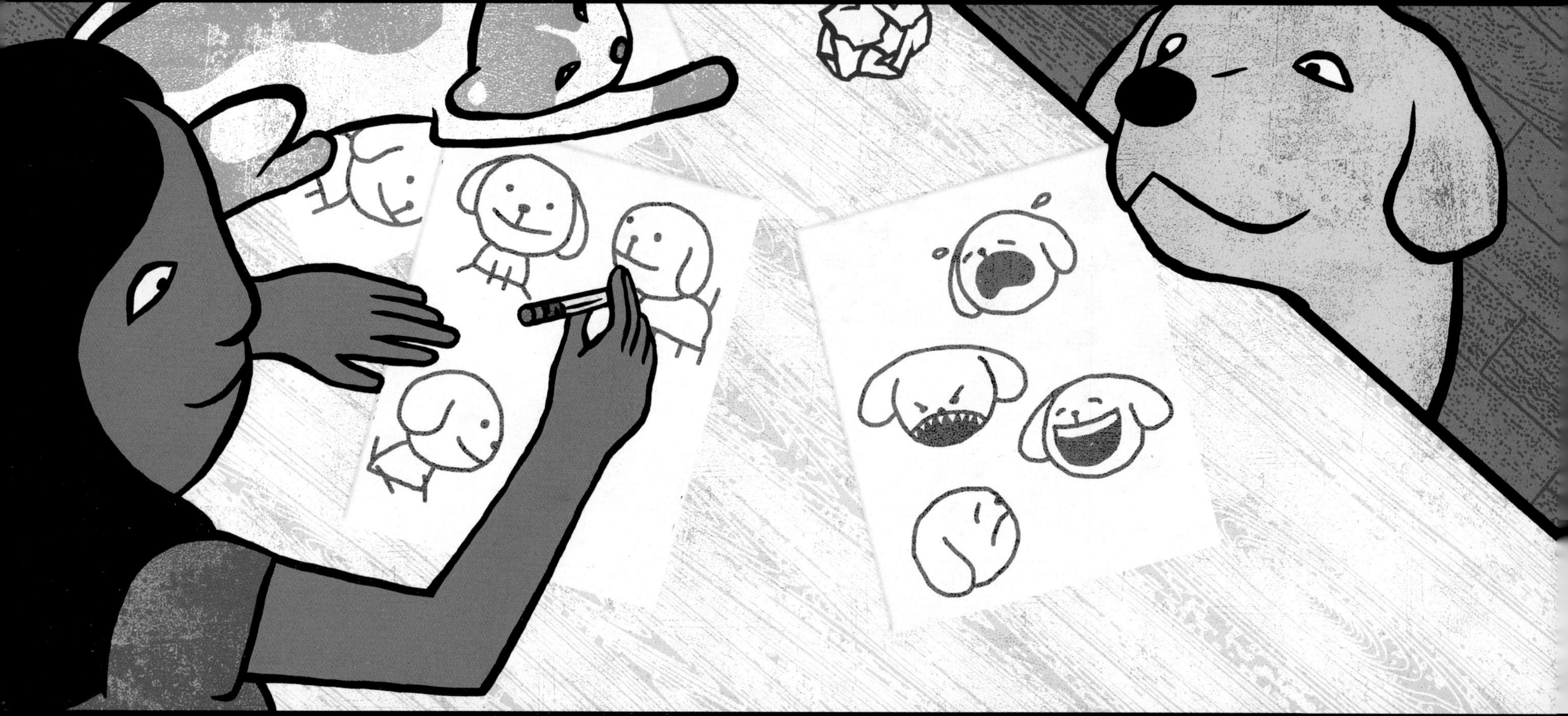

Writing Your Own Graphic Novel

by Trisha Speed Shaskan
illustrated by Stephen Shaskan

PICTURE WINDOW BOOKS
a capstone imprint

Special thanks to our adviser for his expertise:
Terry Flaherty, PhD, Professor of English
Minnesota State University, Mankato

Editor: Jill Kalz
Designer: Nathan Gassman
Production Specialist: Jane Klenk
The illustrations in this book were created digitally.

Picture Window Books
1710 Roe Crest Drive
North Mankato, MN 56003
www.capstonepub.com

All books published by Picture Window Books
are manufactured with paper containing at least
10 percent post-consumer waste.

Library of Congress Cataloging-in-Publication Data
Shaskan, Trisha Speed, 1973–
  Art panels, bam! speech bubbles, pow!: writing your own graphic novel
by Trisha Speed Shaskan ; illustrated by Stephen Shaskan.
    p. cm. — (Writer's toolbox)
Includes index.
ISBN 978-1-4048-6016-2 (library binding)
ISBN 978-1-4048-6393-4 (paperback)
1. Graphic novels—Authorship—Juvenile literature. I. Shaskan,
Stephen. II. Title.
  PN6710.S47 2010
  741.5'1—dc22   2010000887

Printed in the United States of America in North Mankato, Minnesota.
022015
008751R

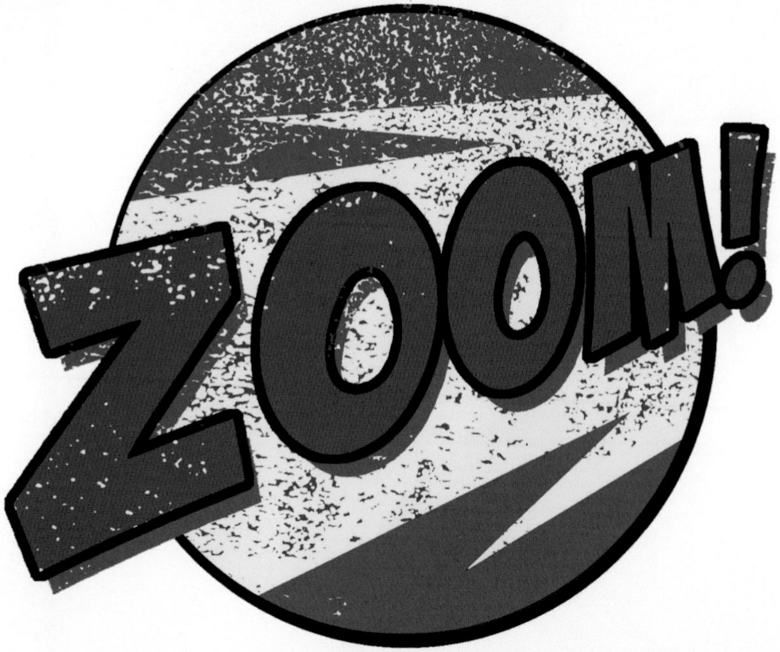
ZOOM!

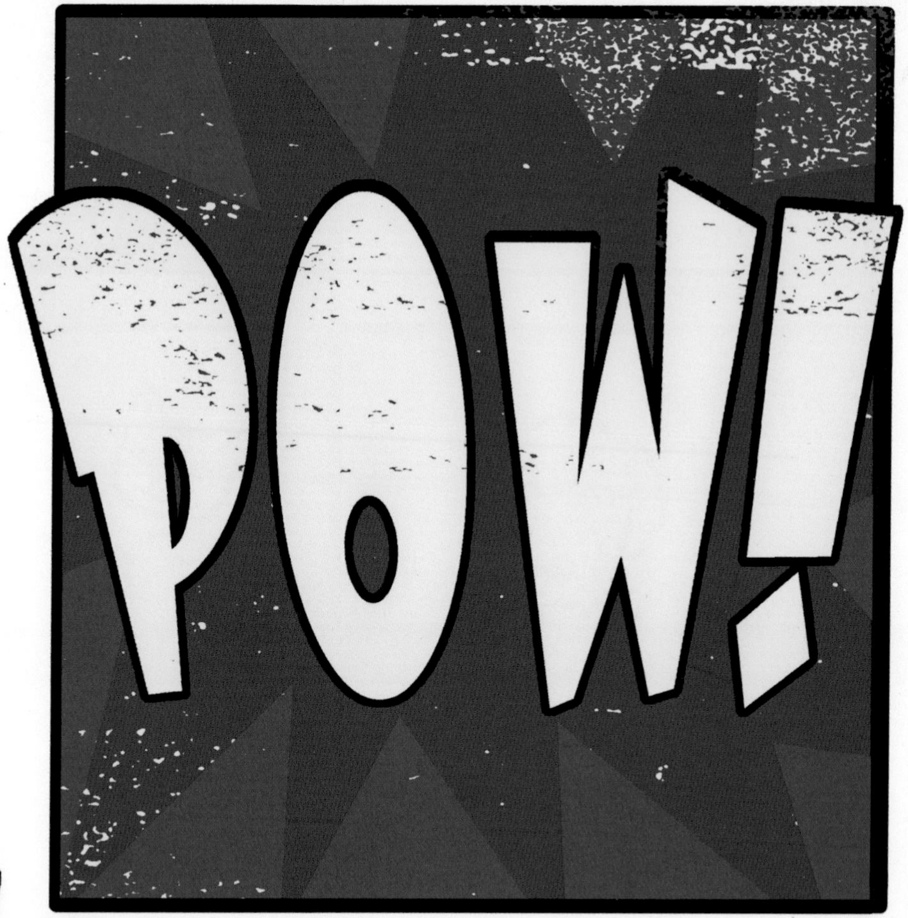
POW!

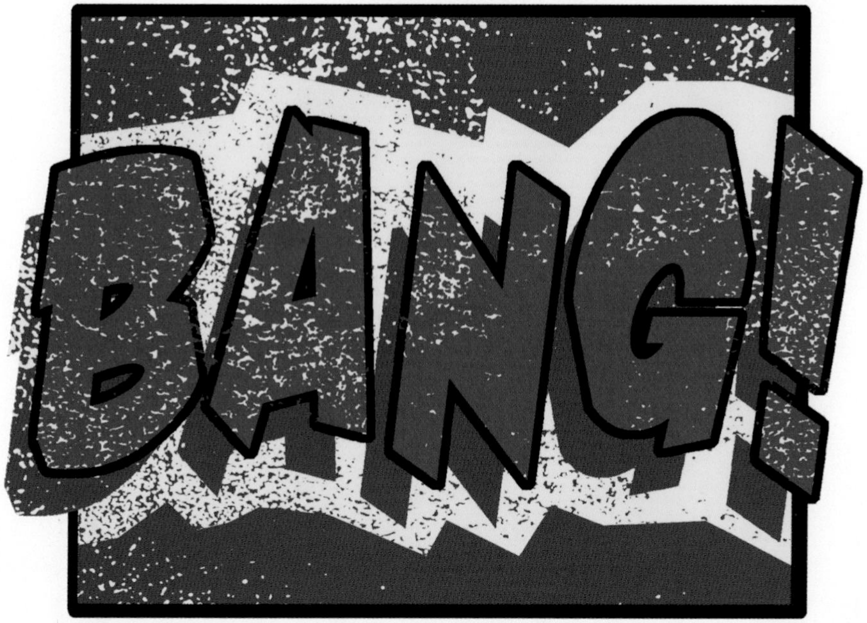
BANG!

These words come to mind when you think of a graphic novel. That's because graphic novels are all about **action!**

A graphic novel is a story told with paneled illustrations. In other words, it's a story told in a series of pictures. When creating a graphic novel, you need to think about how words and pictures can work together.

Let's get started!

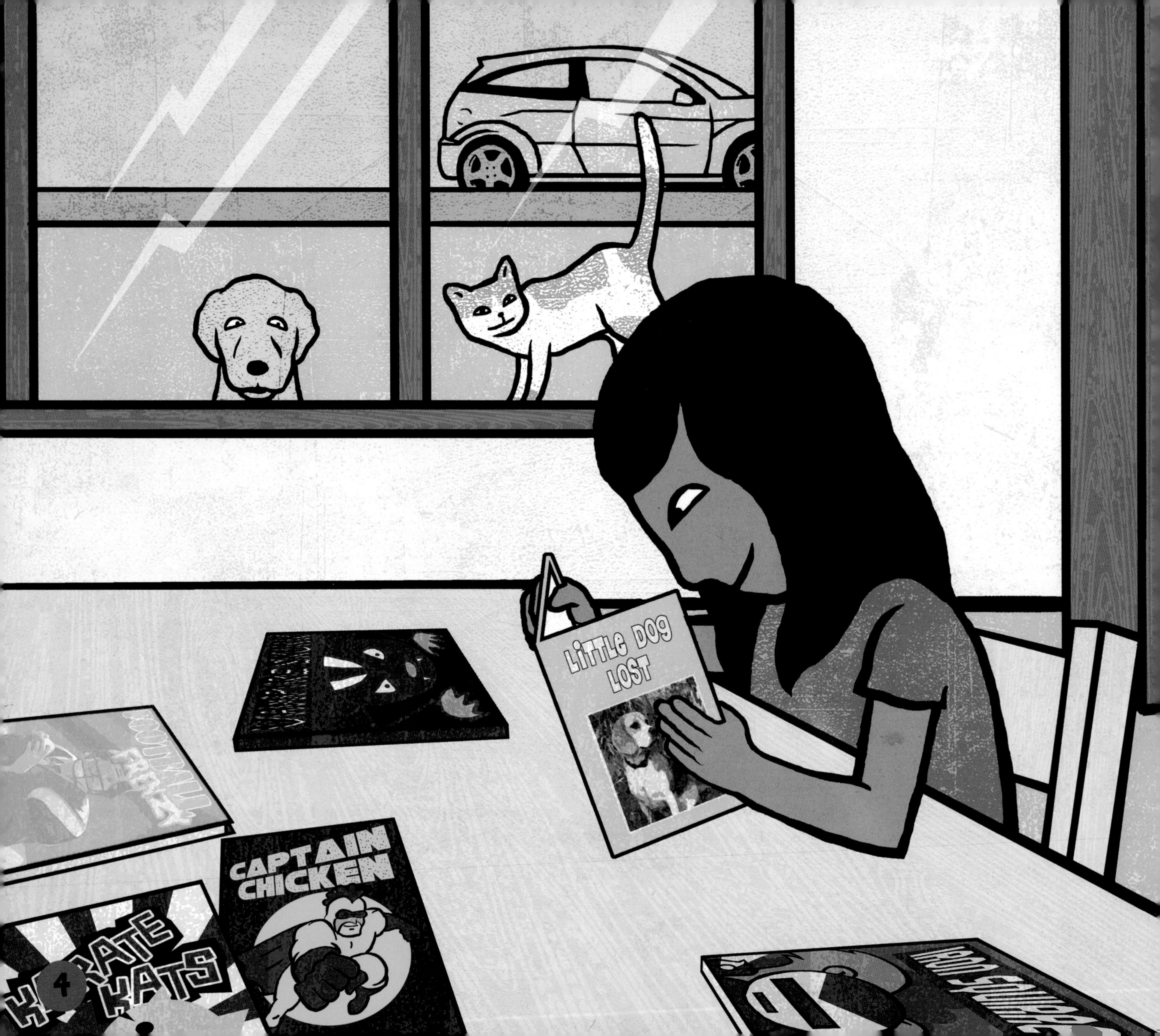
LITTLE DOG LOST
FOOTBALL FRENZY
CAPTAIN CHICKEN
KARATE KATS

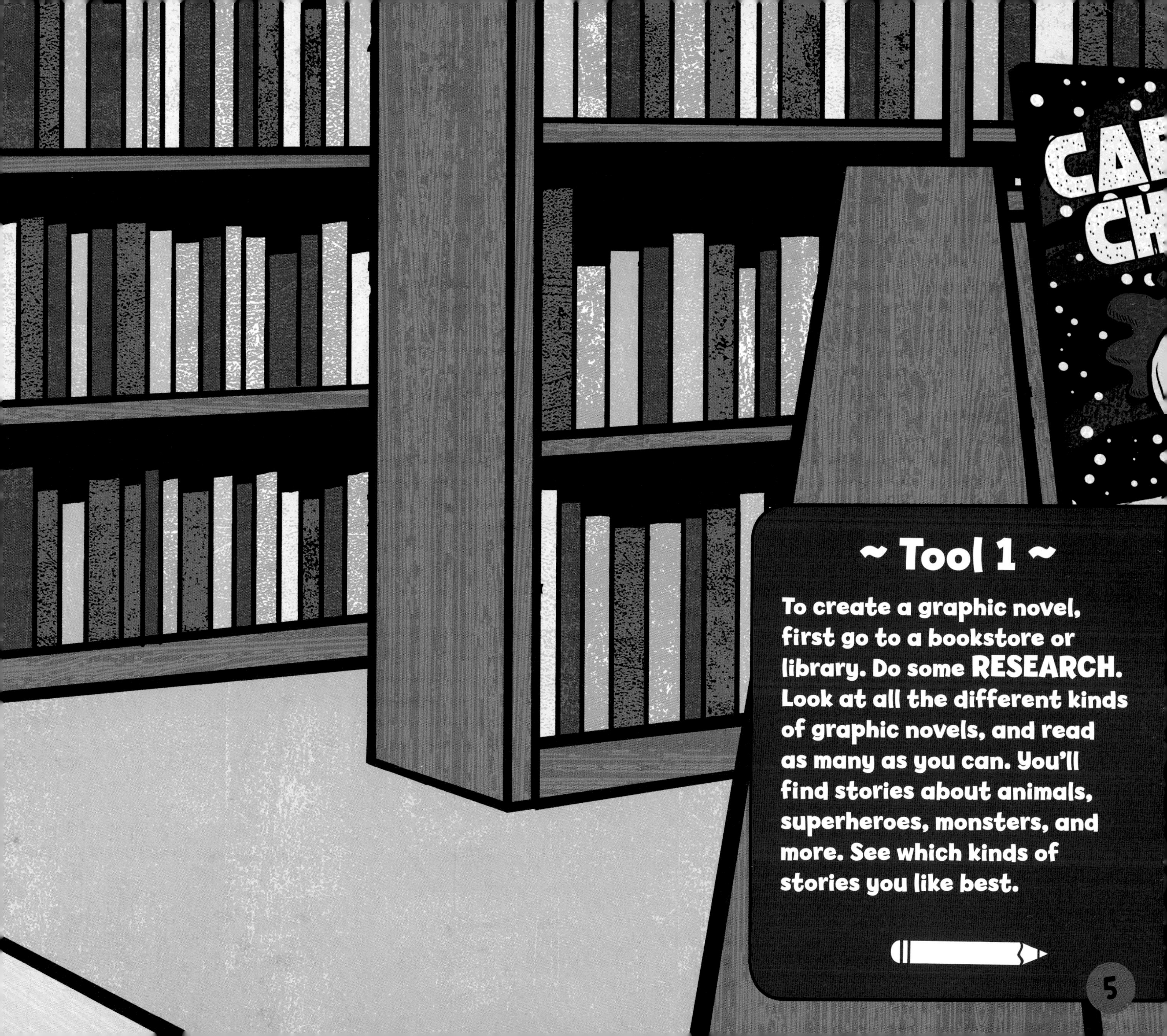

~ Tool 1 ~

To create a graphic novel, first go to a bookstore or library. Do some **RESEARCH.** Look at all the different kinds of graphic novels, and read as many as you can. You'll find stories about animals, superheroes, monsters, and more. See which kinds of stories you like best.

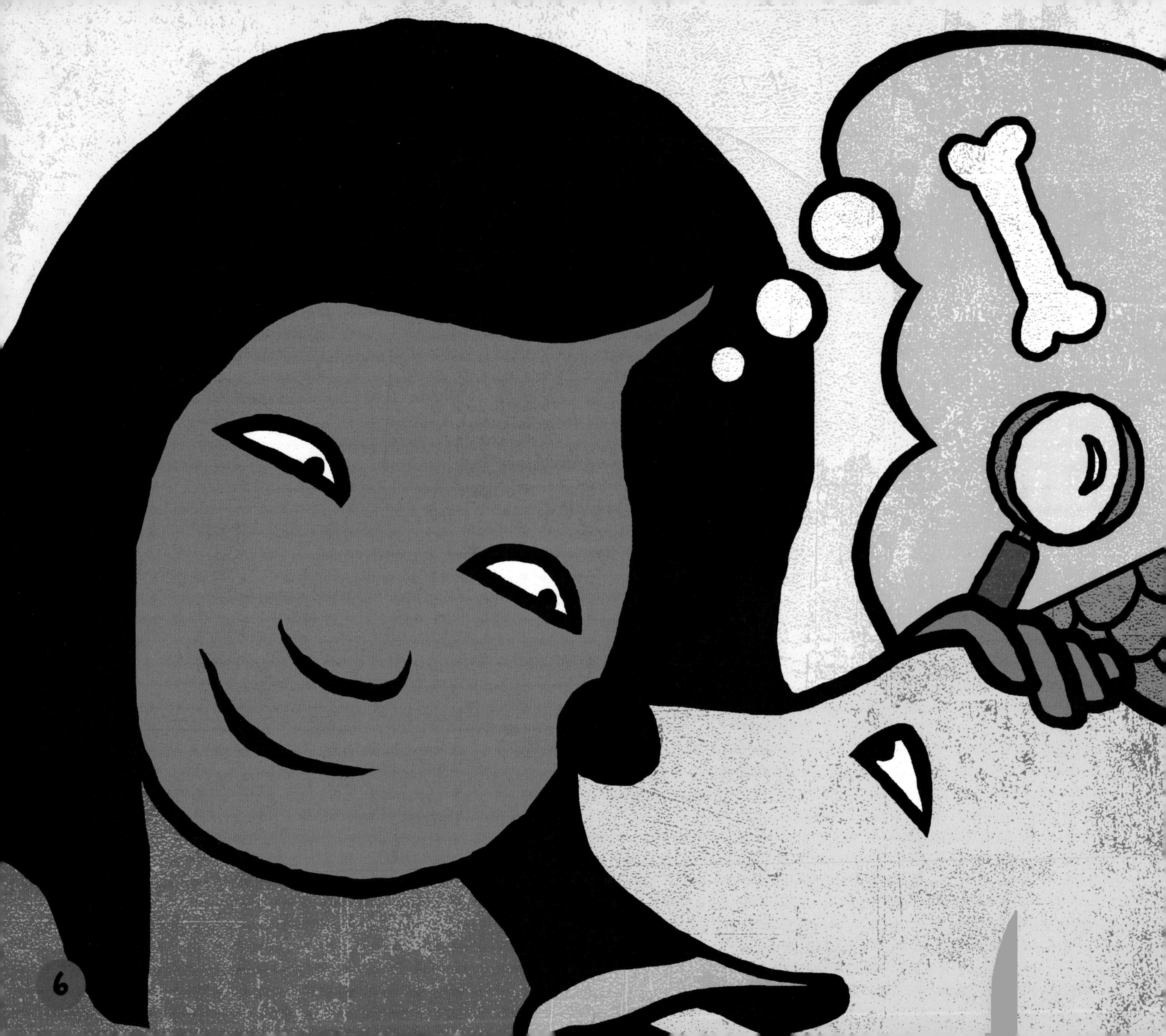

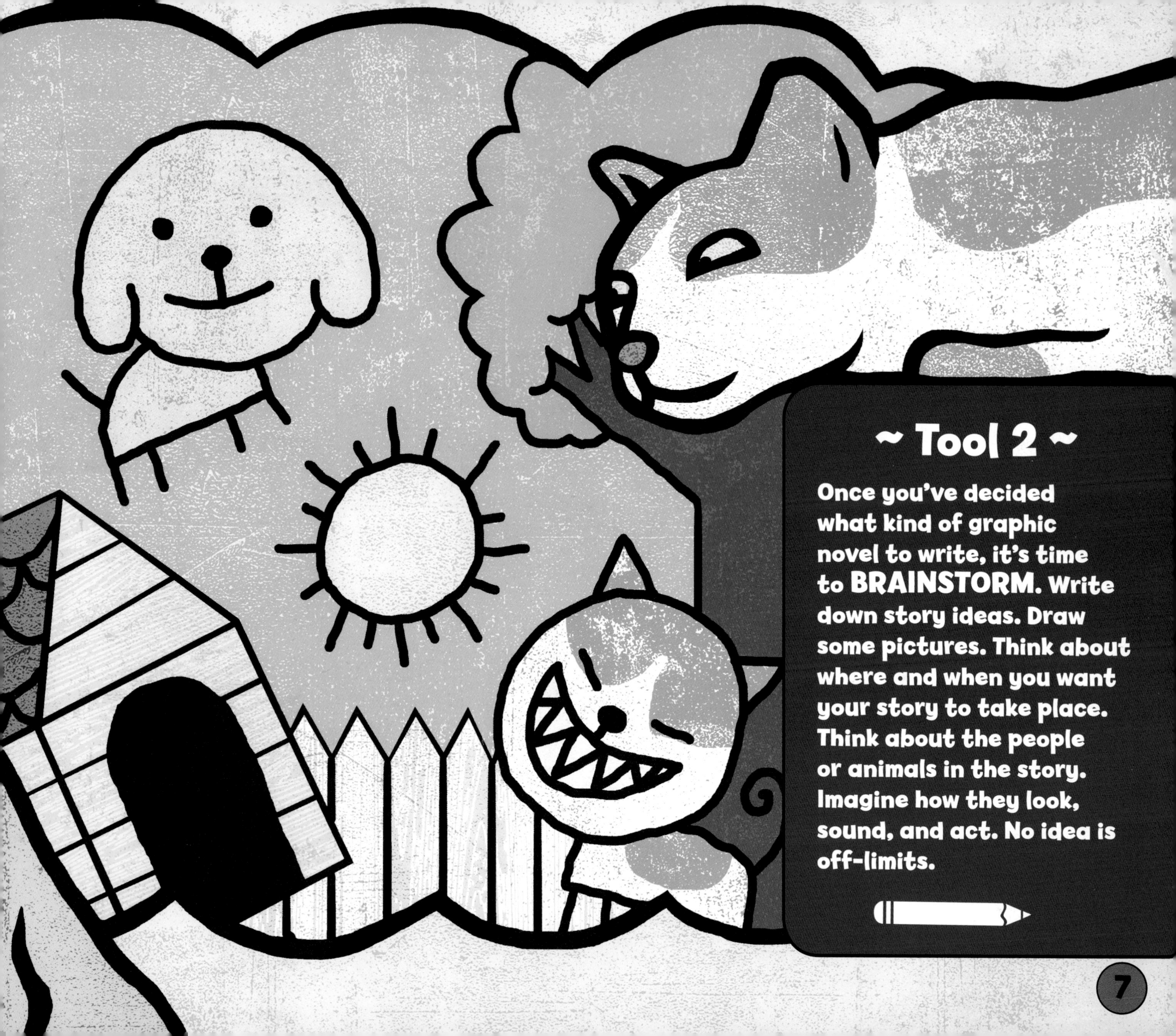

~ Tool 2 ~

Once you've decided what kind of graphic novel to write, it's time to **BRAINSTORM**. Write down story ideas. Draw some pictures. Think about where and when you want your story to take place. Think about the people or animals in the story. Imagine how they look, sound, and act. No idea is off-limits.

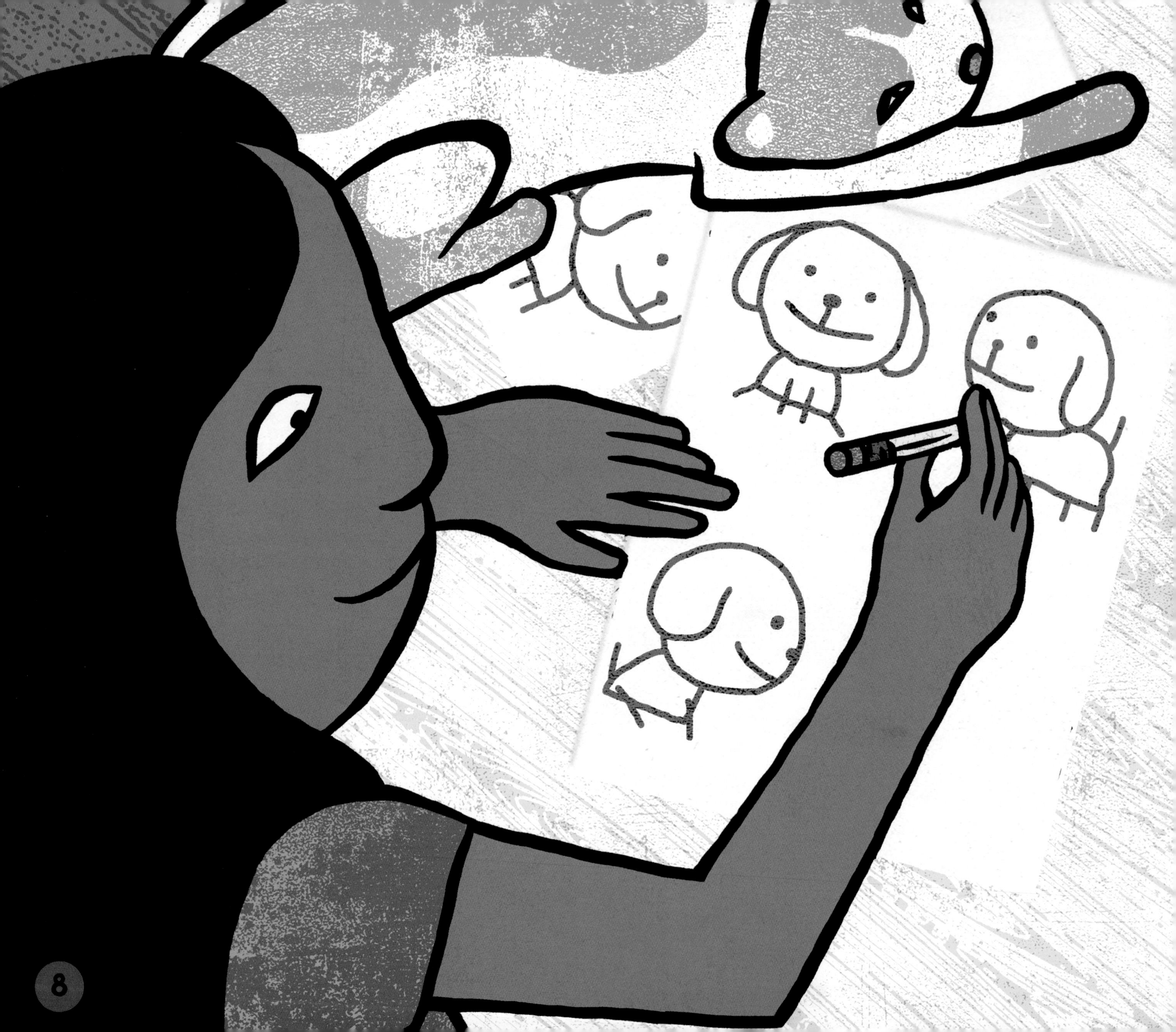

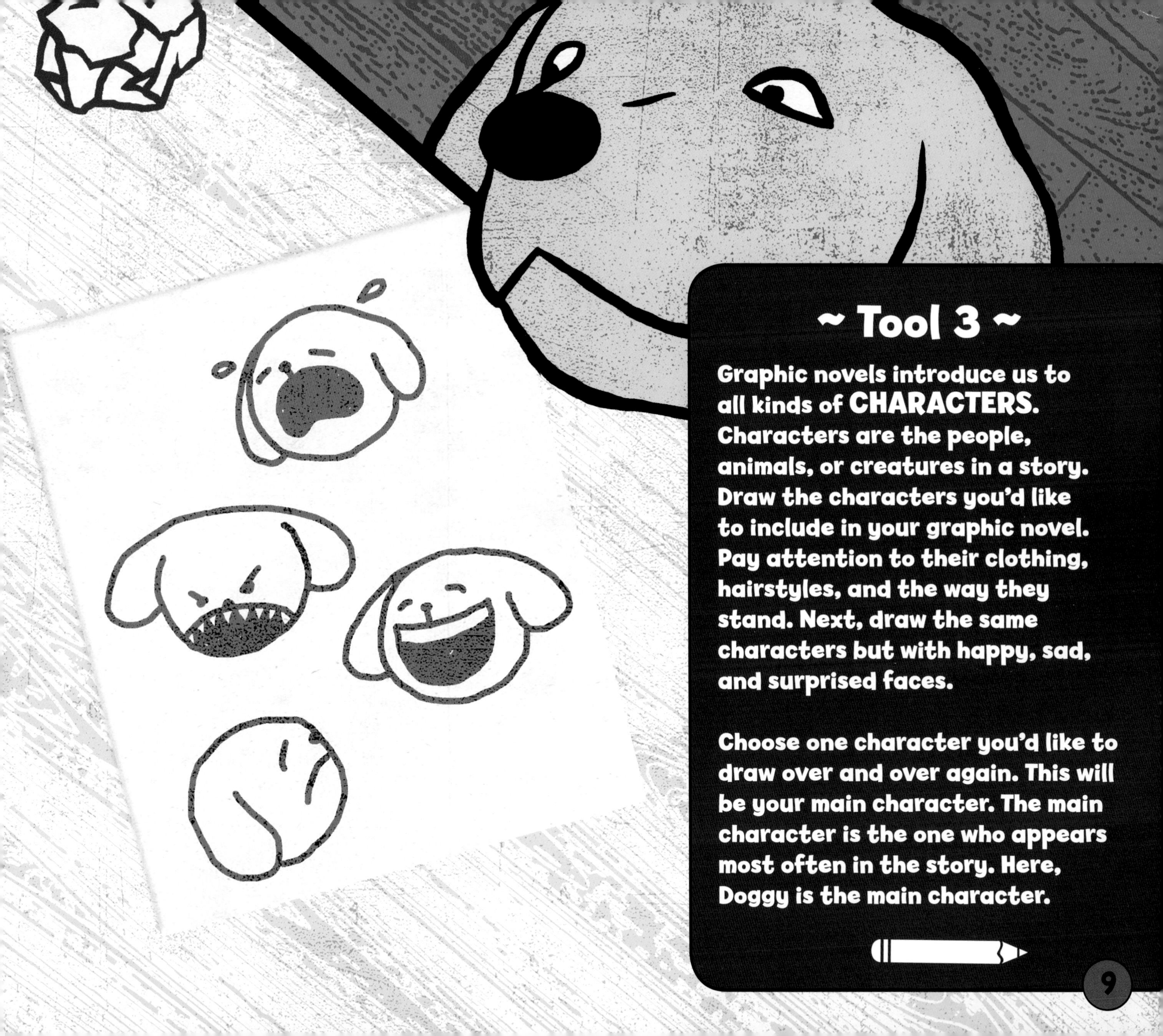

~ Tool 3 ~

Graphic novels introduce us to all kinds of **CHARACTERS.** Characters are the people, animals, or creatures in a story. Draw the characters you'd like to include in your graphic novel. Pay attention to their clothing, hairstyles, and the way they stand. Next, draw the same characters but with happy, sad, and surprised faces.

Choose one character you'd like to draw over and over again. This will be your main character. The main character is the one who appears most often in the story. Here, Doggy is the main character.

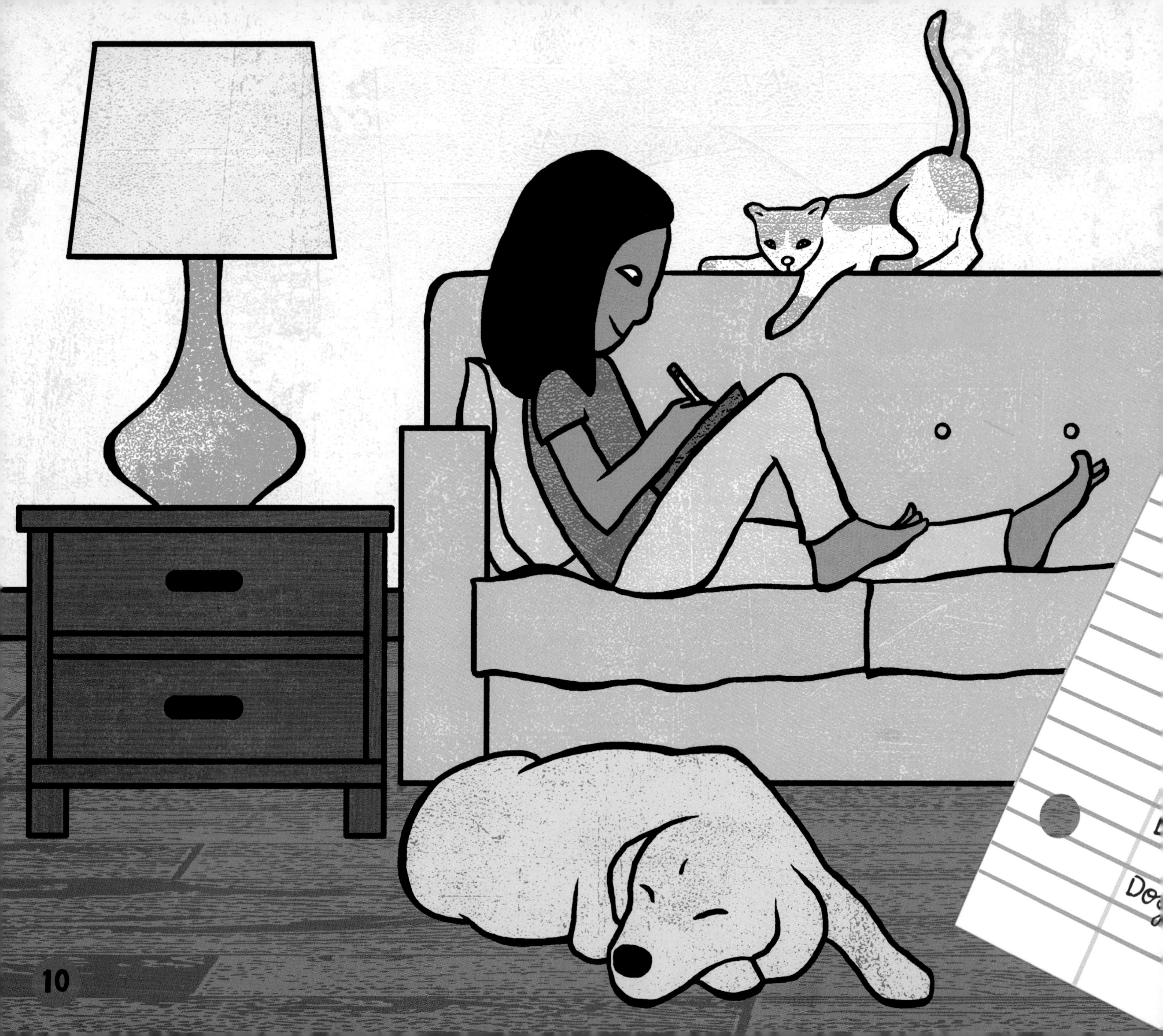

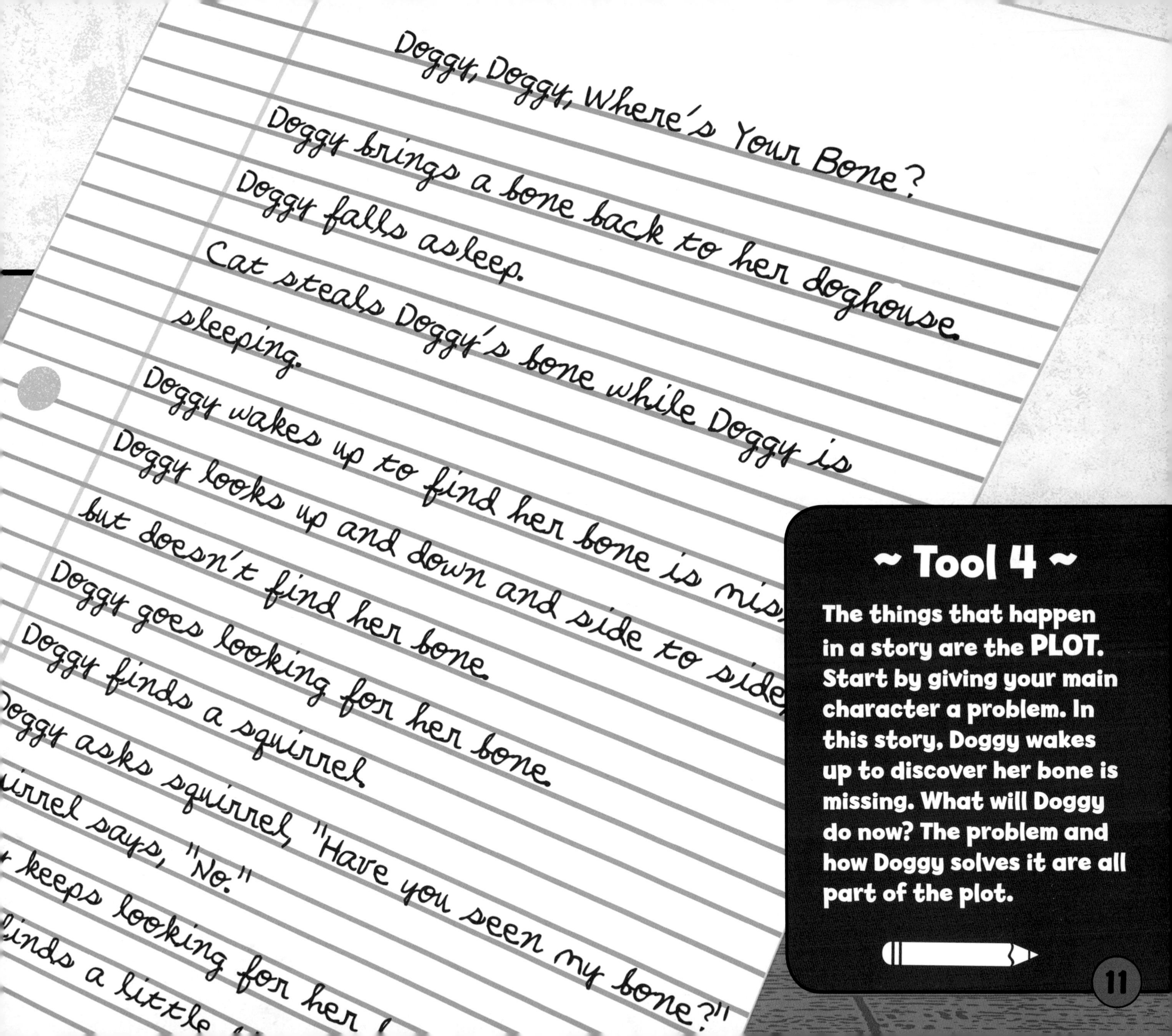
Doggy, Doggy, Where's Your Bone?
Doggy brings a bone back to her doghouse.
Doggy falls asleep.
Cat steals Doggy's bone while Doggy is
sleeping.
Doggy wakes up to find her bone is mis
Doggy looks up and down and side to side
but doesn't find her bone.
Doggy goes looking for her bone.
Doggy finds a squirrel.
oggy asks squirrel, "Have you seen my bone?"
irrel says, "No."
keeps looking for her
inds a little

~ Tool 4 ~

The things that happen in a story are the PLOT. Start by giving your main character a problem. In this story, Doggy wakes up to discover her bone is missing. What will Doggy do now? The problem and how Doggy solves it are all part of the plot.

~ Tool 5 ~

It's a good idea to know your entire story before moving to this next step. **THUMBNAIL SKETCHES** are small, quick drawings. They are used to fit your story into an order, or sequence. When doing thumbnail sketches, think about making the action of the story clear. Sketches that show action are the most interesting. Be sure to leave space for the words.

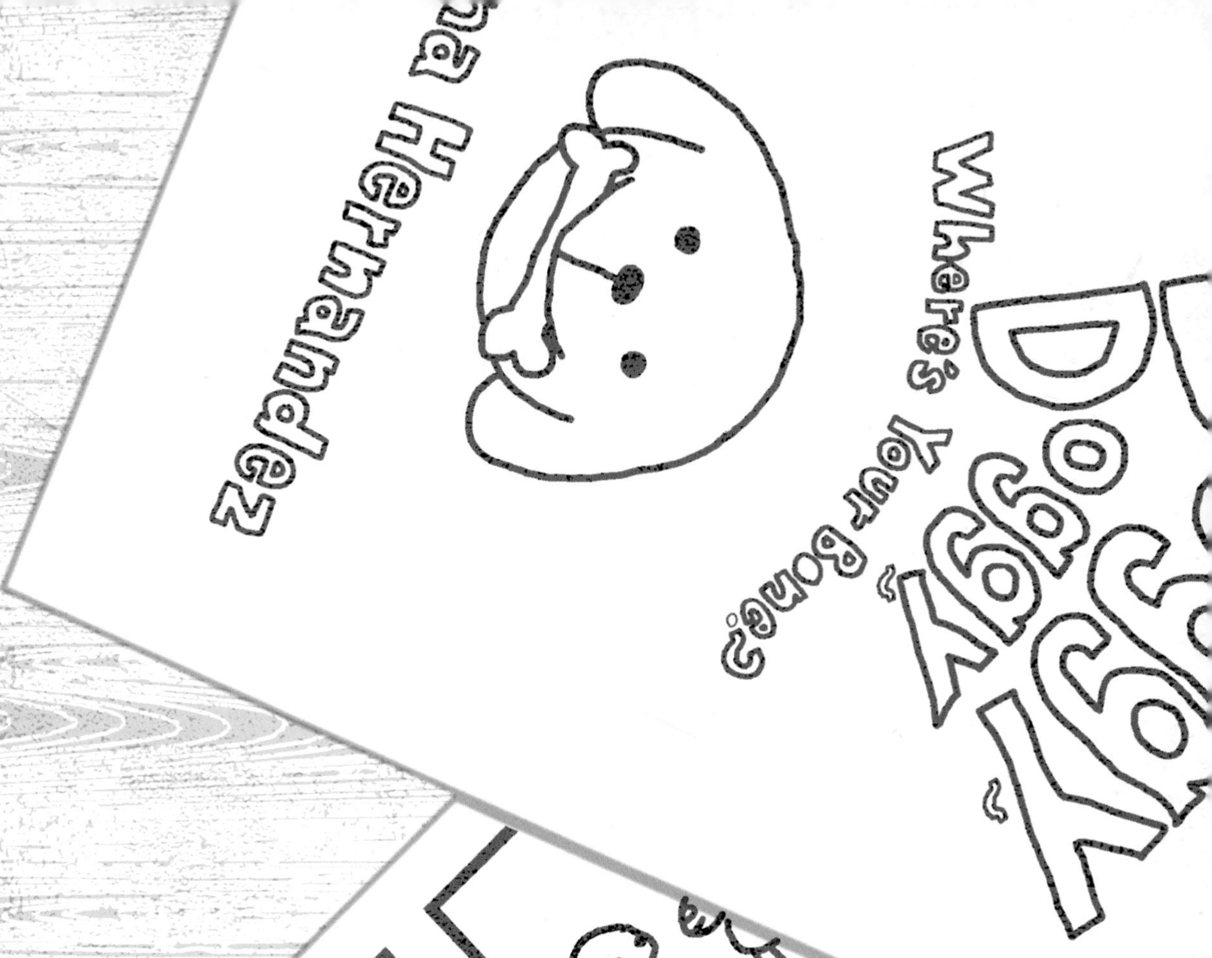
Where's Your Bone?

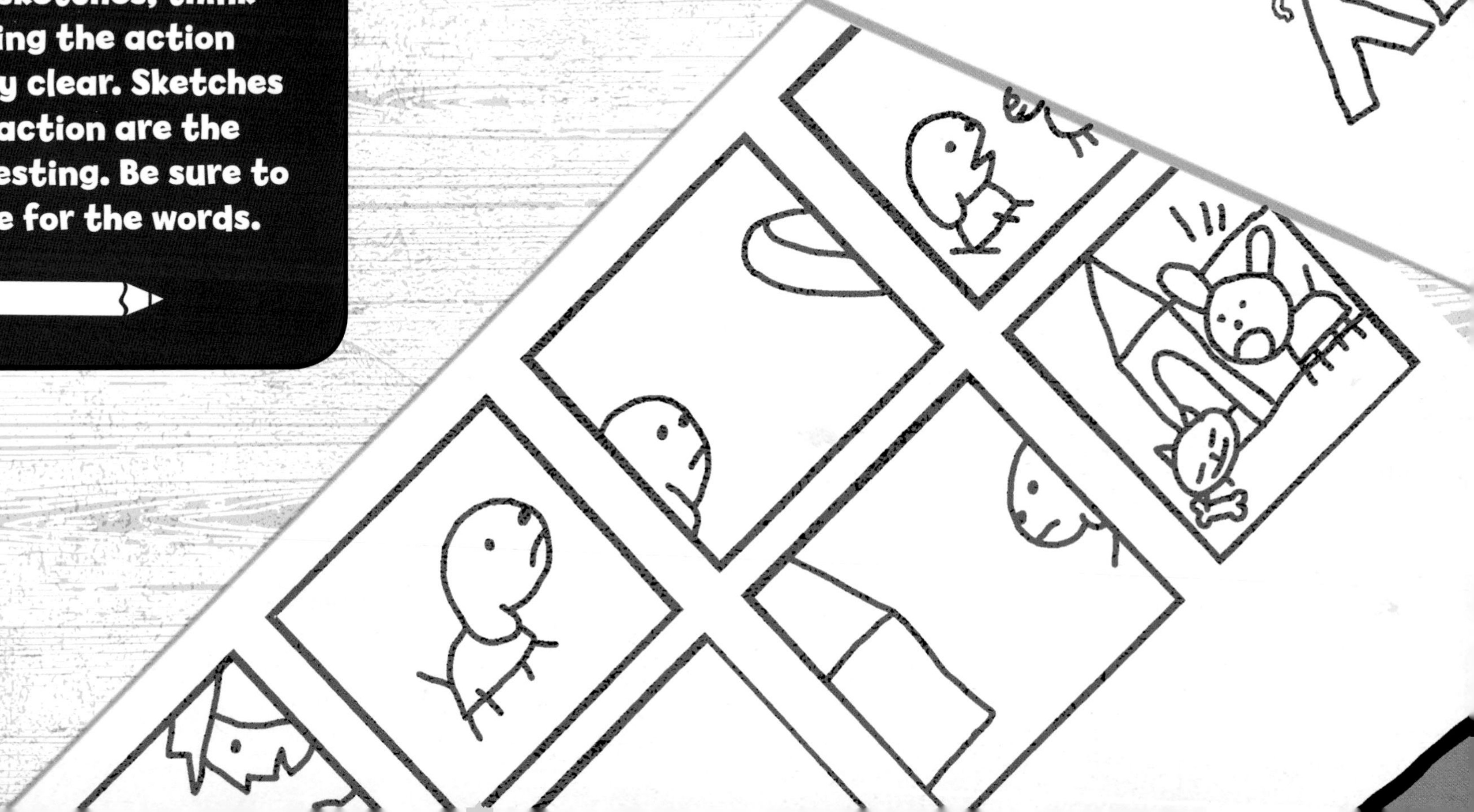

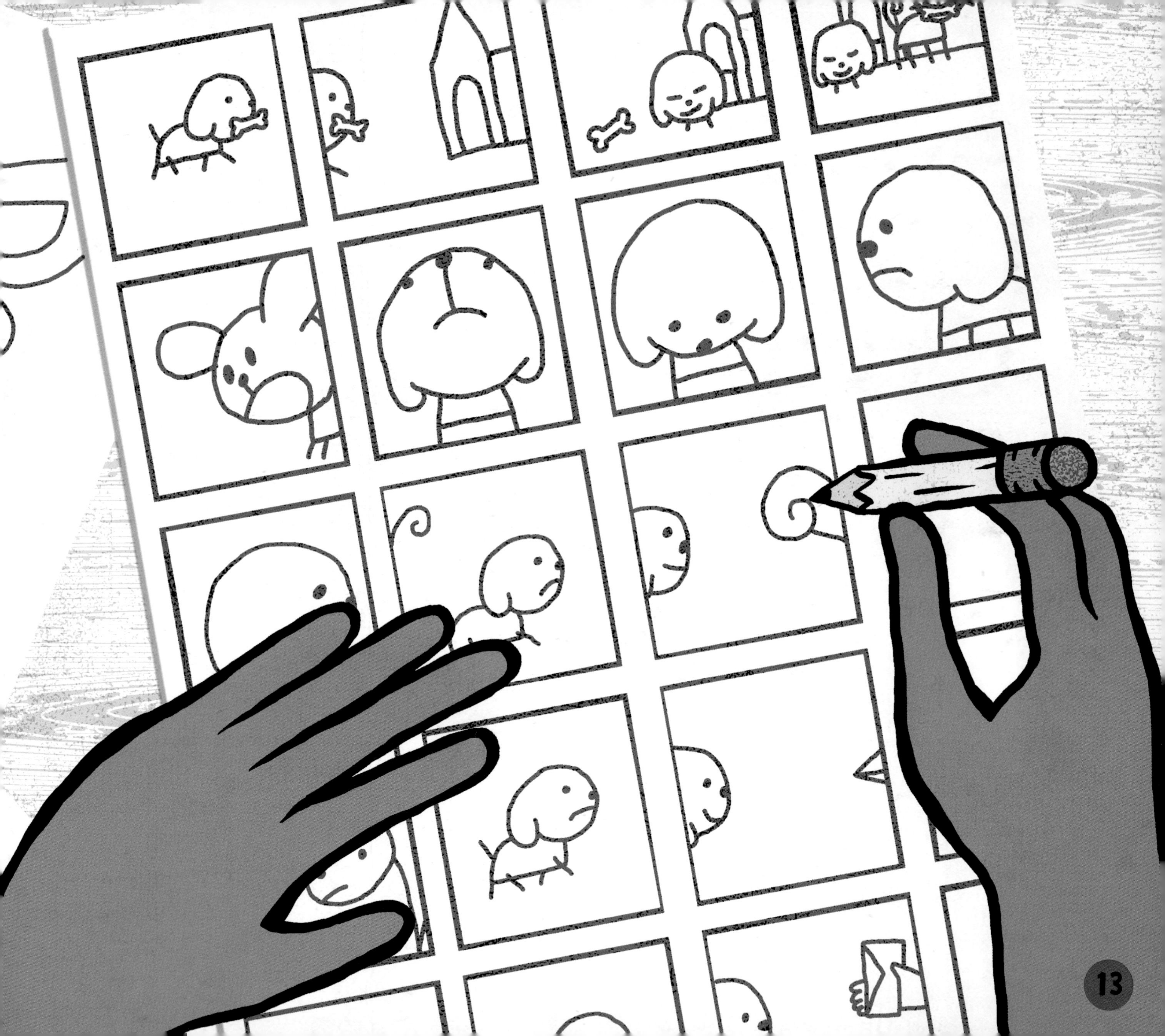

Deciding when to use pictures and words is important when creating thumbnail sketches. Sometimes you can move the story along with just a picture. Sometimes just words will do. But it's often best when the pictures and words work together. Here, Squirrel shrugs his shoulders as he says, "No."

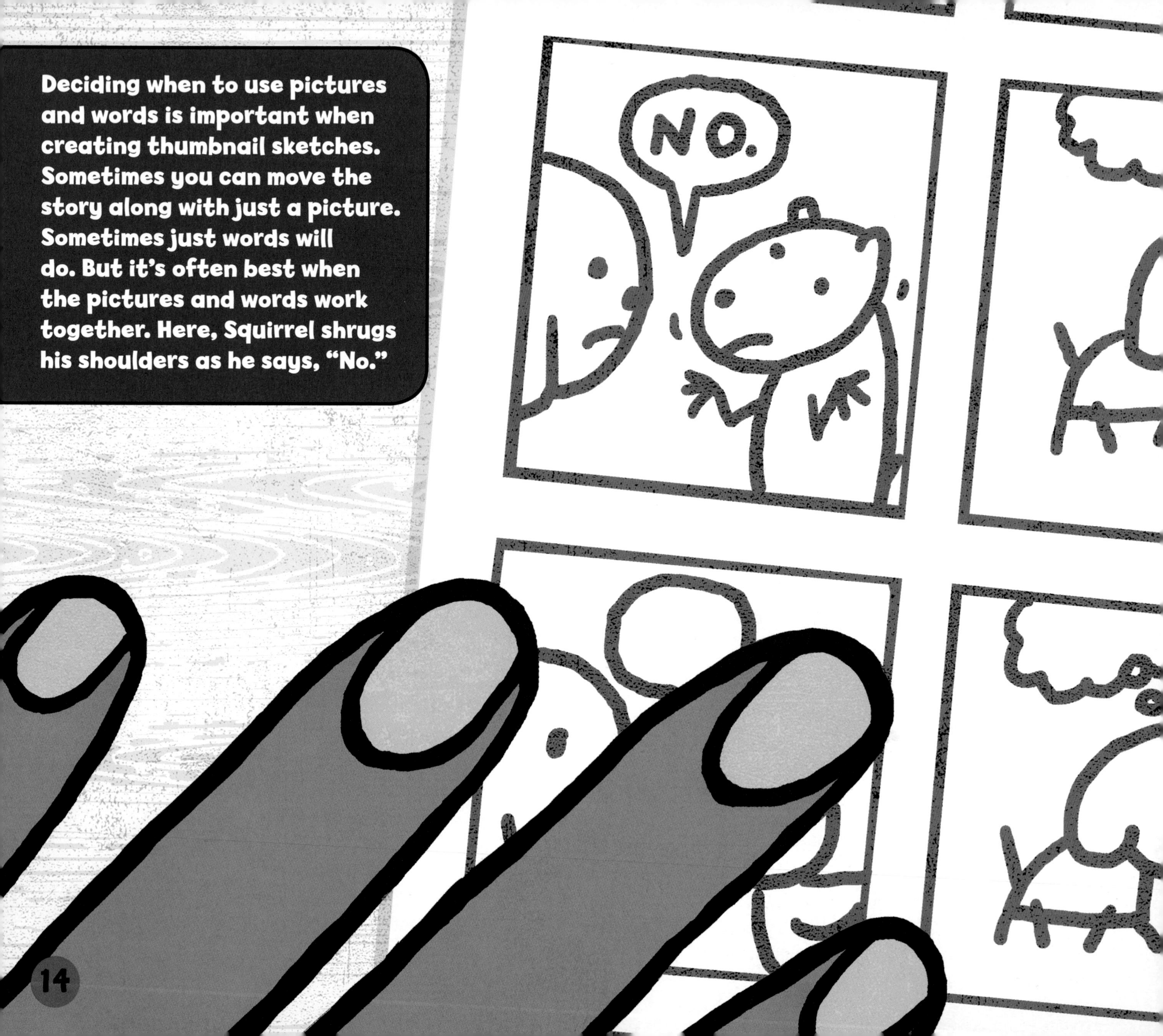
NO.

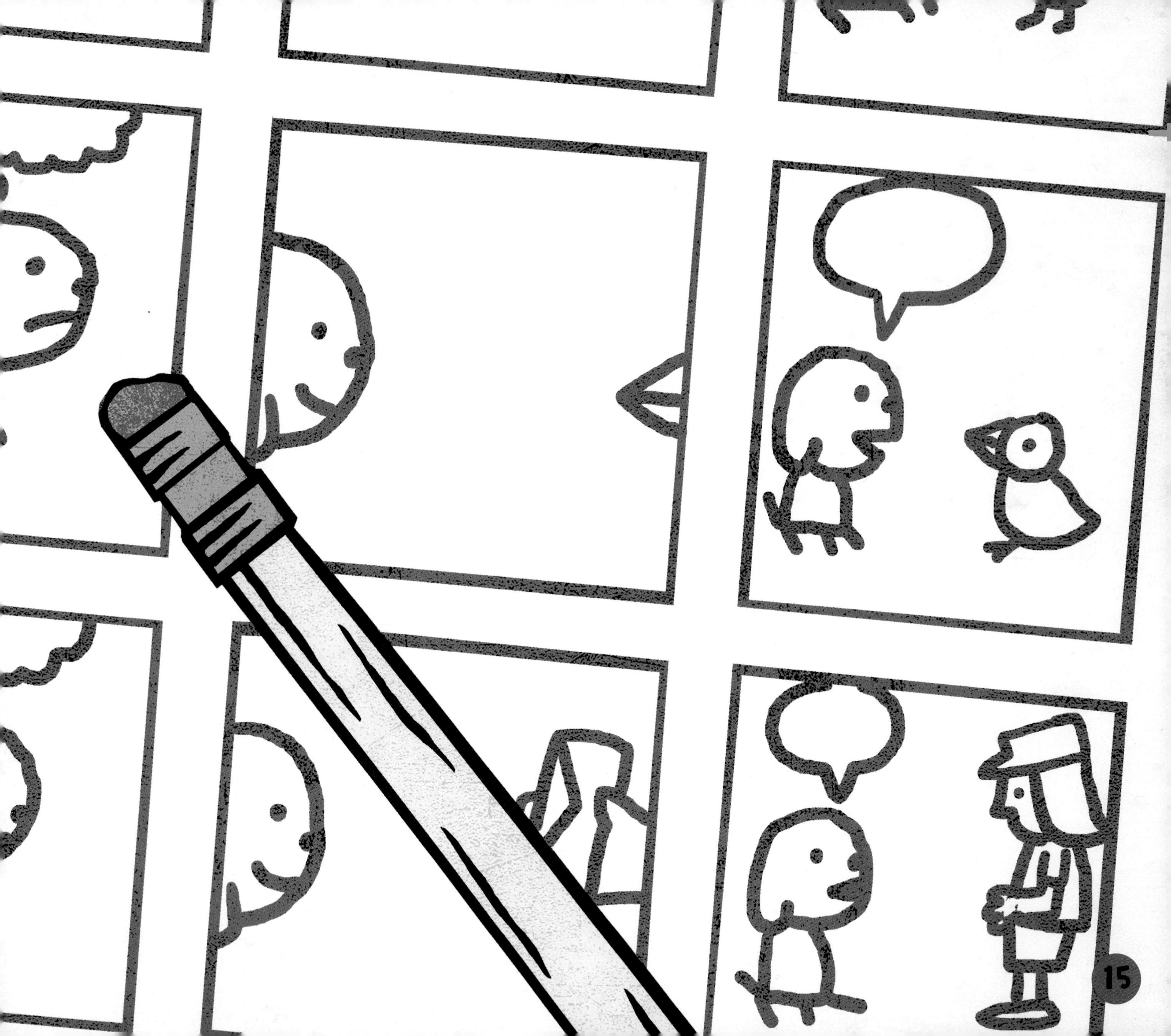

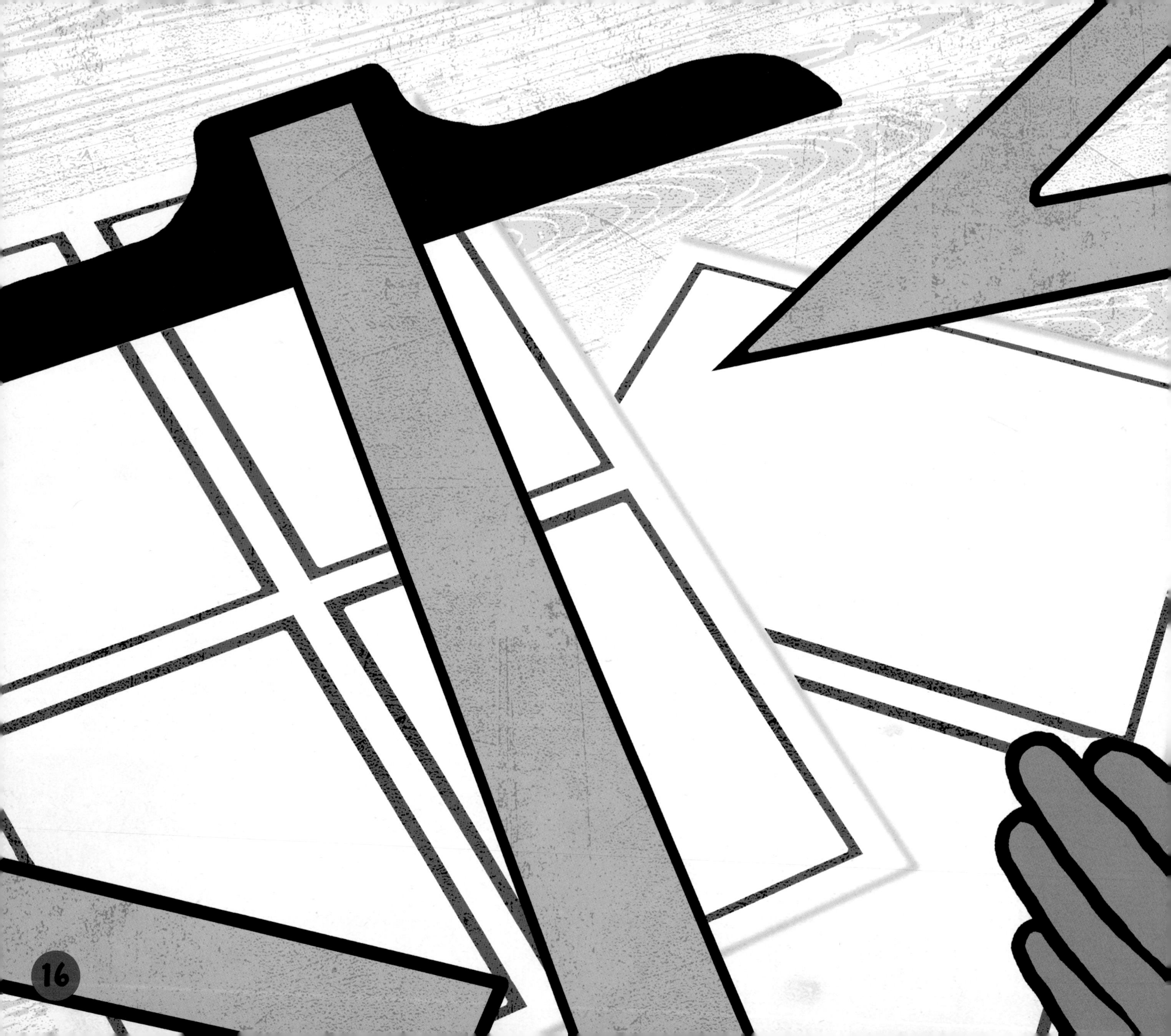

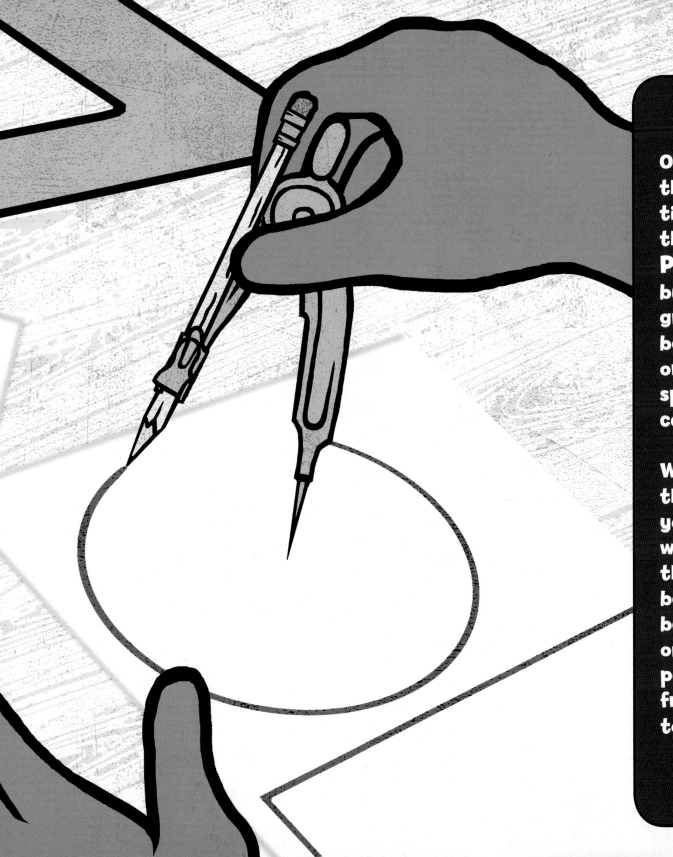

~ Tool 6 ~

Once you've drawn your thumbnail sketches, it's time to lay them out on the page. To do this, make **PANELS.** Panels are the building blocks of the graphic novel. They can be squares, rectangles, or any other shape. The space between panels is called the gutter.

When you create panels, think about how many of your thumbnail sketches will fit on a page. Your thumbnail sketches will become panels. There can be any number of panels on a page. Just remember, people will read your novel from left to right and top to bottom.

Next, fill in the panels. Look at your thumbnail sketches. Look at how you've laid out the story. Now get more detailed. One way to fill in the panels is with your characters.

~ Tool 7 ~

Make room for **CAPTIONS** and **BUBBLES** *now*, but fill them in after you've finished your art. Captions, or narrative boxes, explain what's happening in a panel or on a page. Instead of saying "he said" or "she said," use a speech bubble by the character's head. To show what a character is thinking, use a wavy thought bubble.

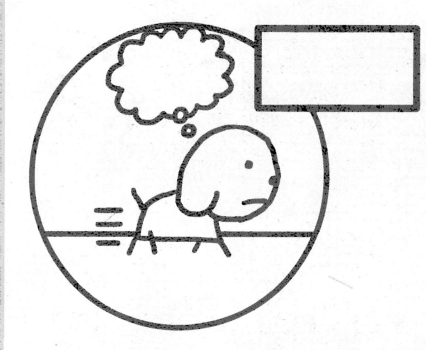

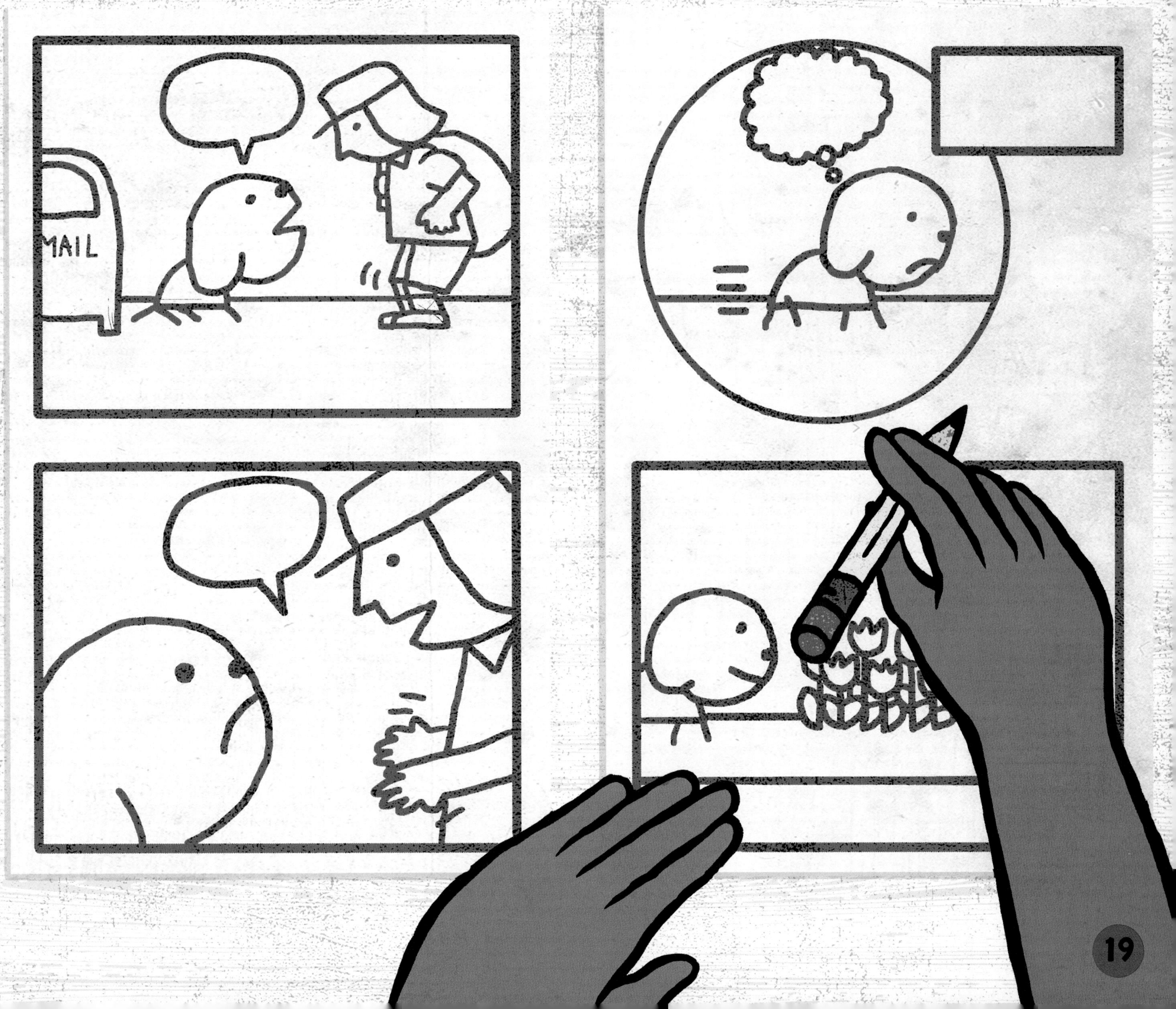
MAIL

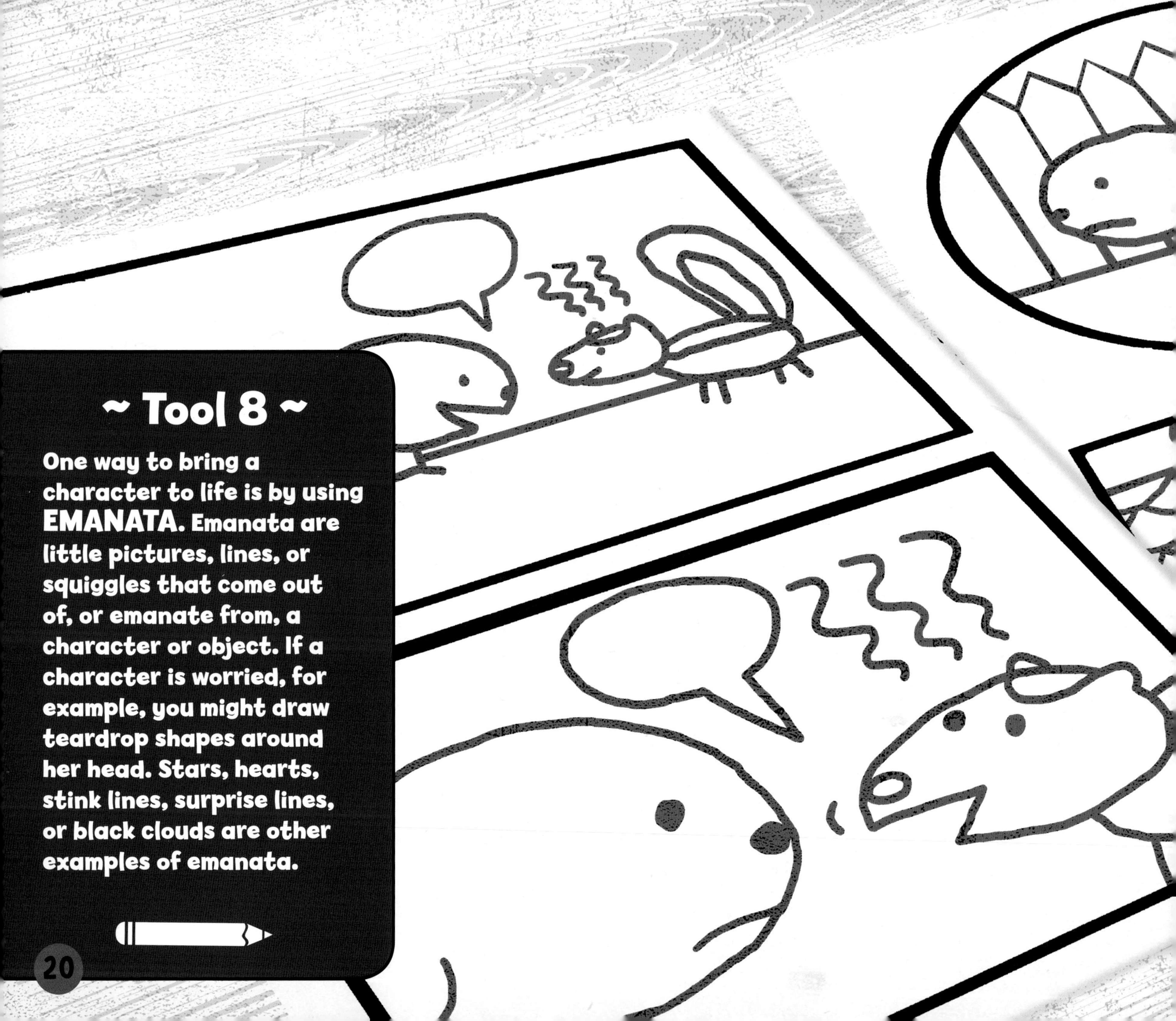

~ Tool 8 ~

One way to bring a character to life is by using EMANATA. Emanata are little pictures, lines, or squiggles that come out of, or emanate from, a character or object. If a character is worried, for example, you might draw teardrop shapes around her head. Stars, hearts, stink lines, surprise lines, or black clouds are other examples of emanata.

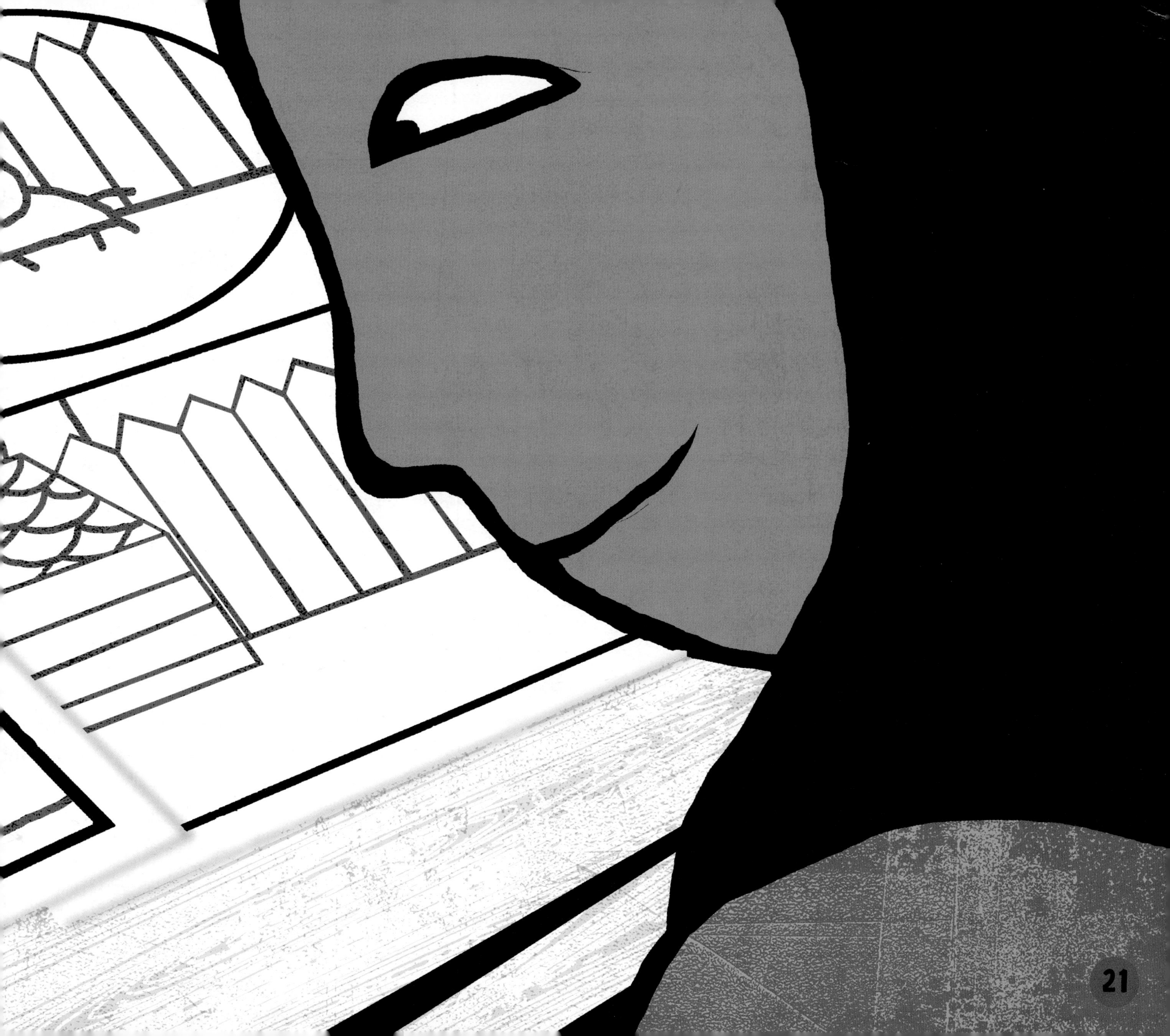

~ Tool 9 ~

Sometimes it's nice to break up your graphic novel with a SPLASH PAGE. A splash page is a full-page illustration. The art isn't divided into panels. Comic books often start with a splash page. A splash page may be used to show an exciting or important point in the story. The moment when Doggy first realizes her bone is missing makes a good splash page.

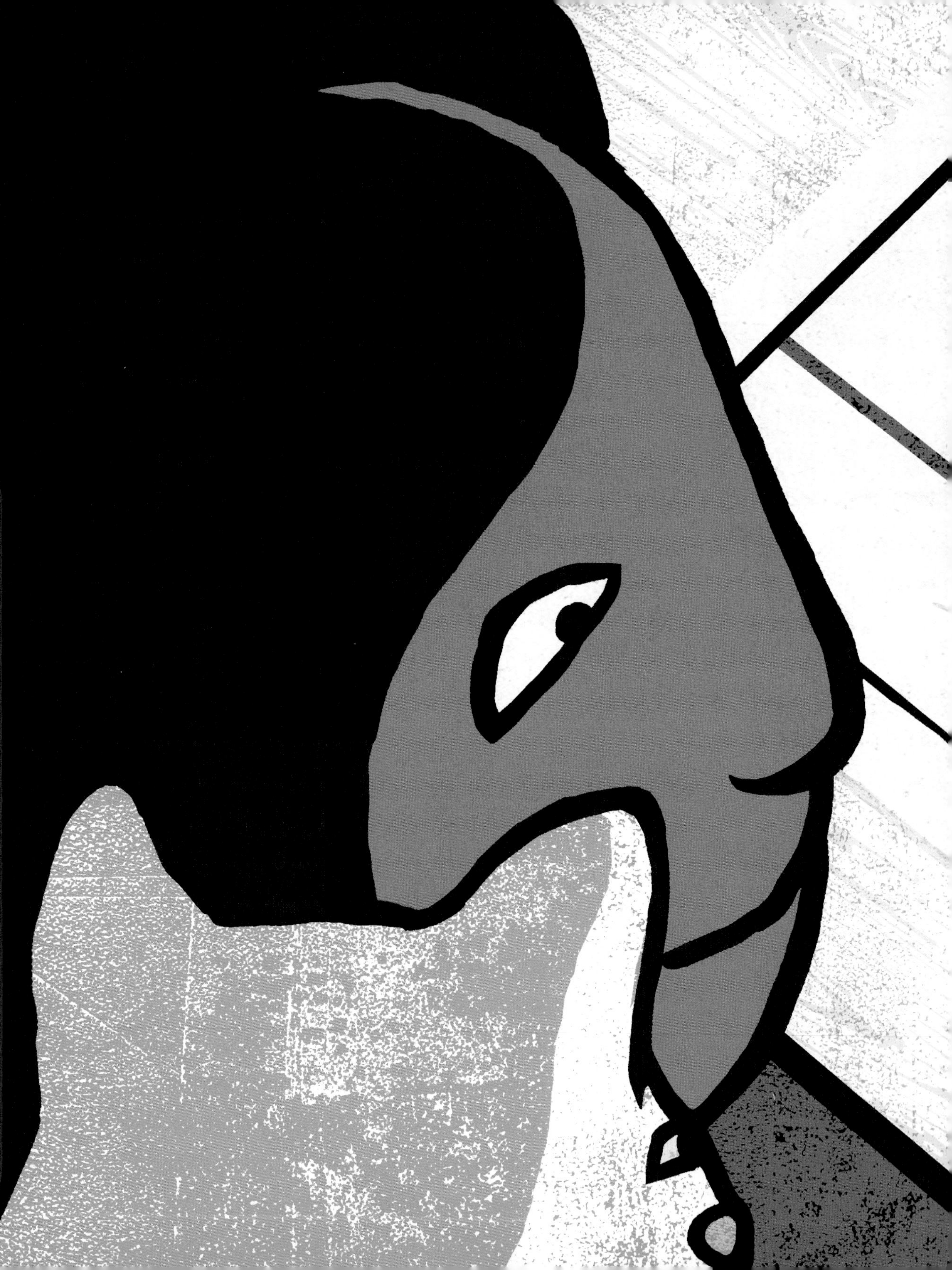

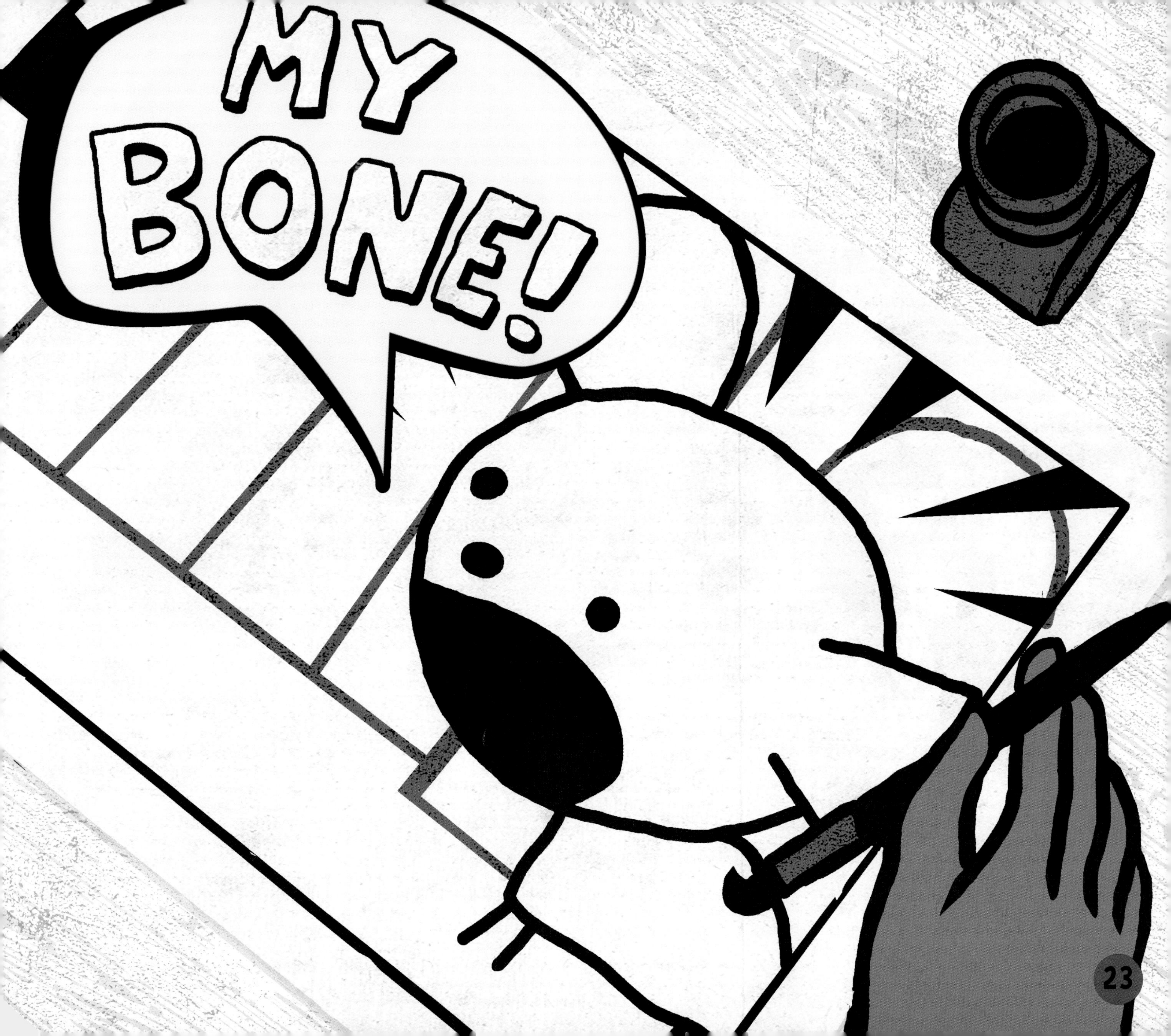
MY BONE!

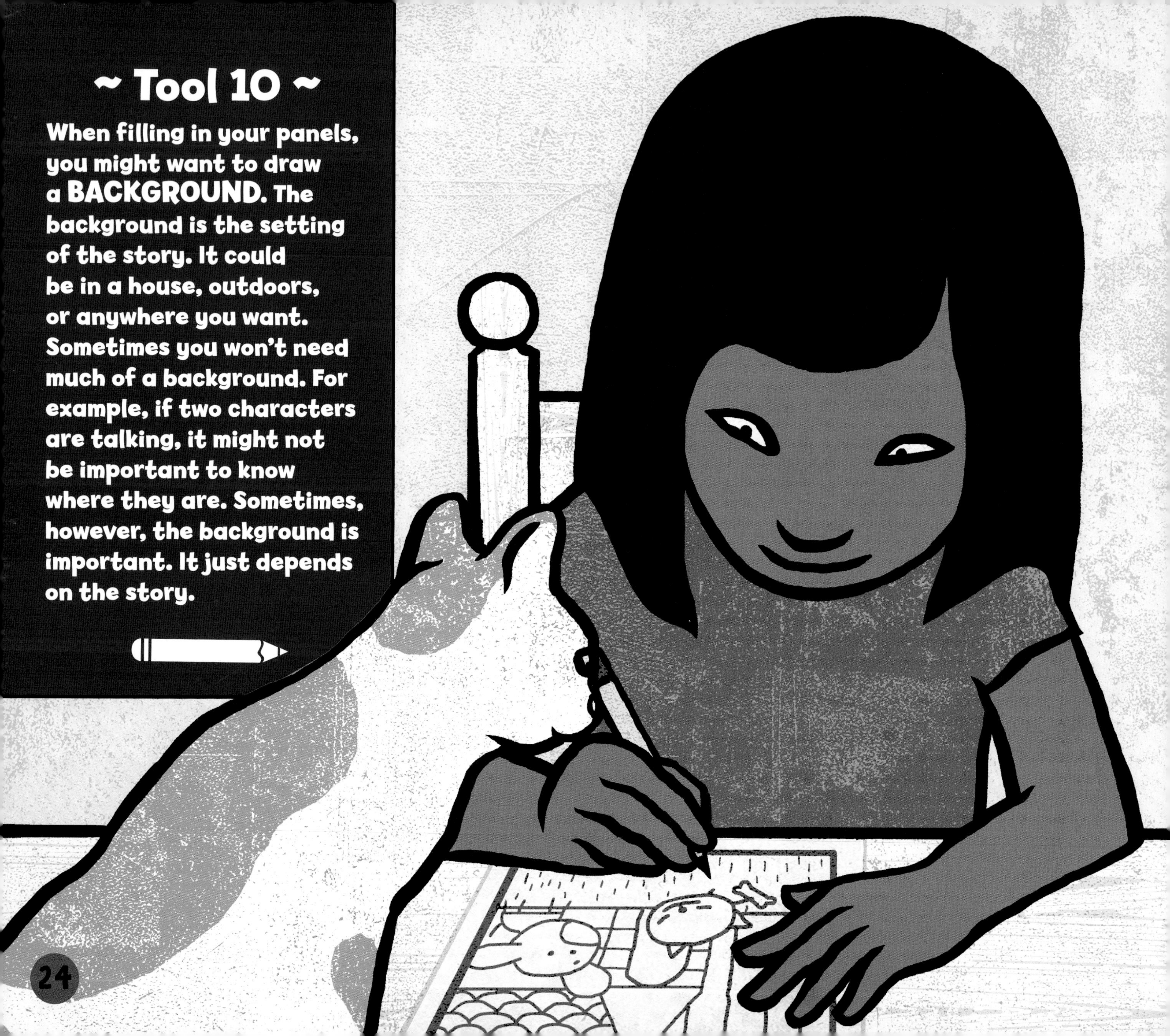

~ Tool 10 ~

When filling in your panels, you might want to draw a BACKGROUND. The background is the setting of the story. It could be in a house, outdoors, or anywhere you want. Sometimes you won't need much of a background. For example, if two characters are talking, it might not be important to know where they are. Sometimes, however, the background is important. It just depends on the story.

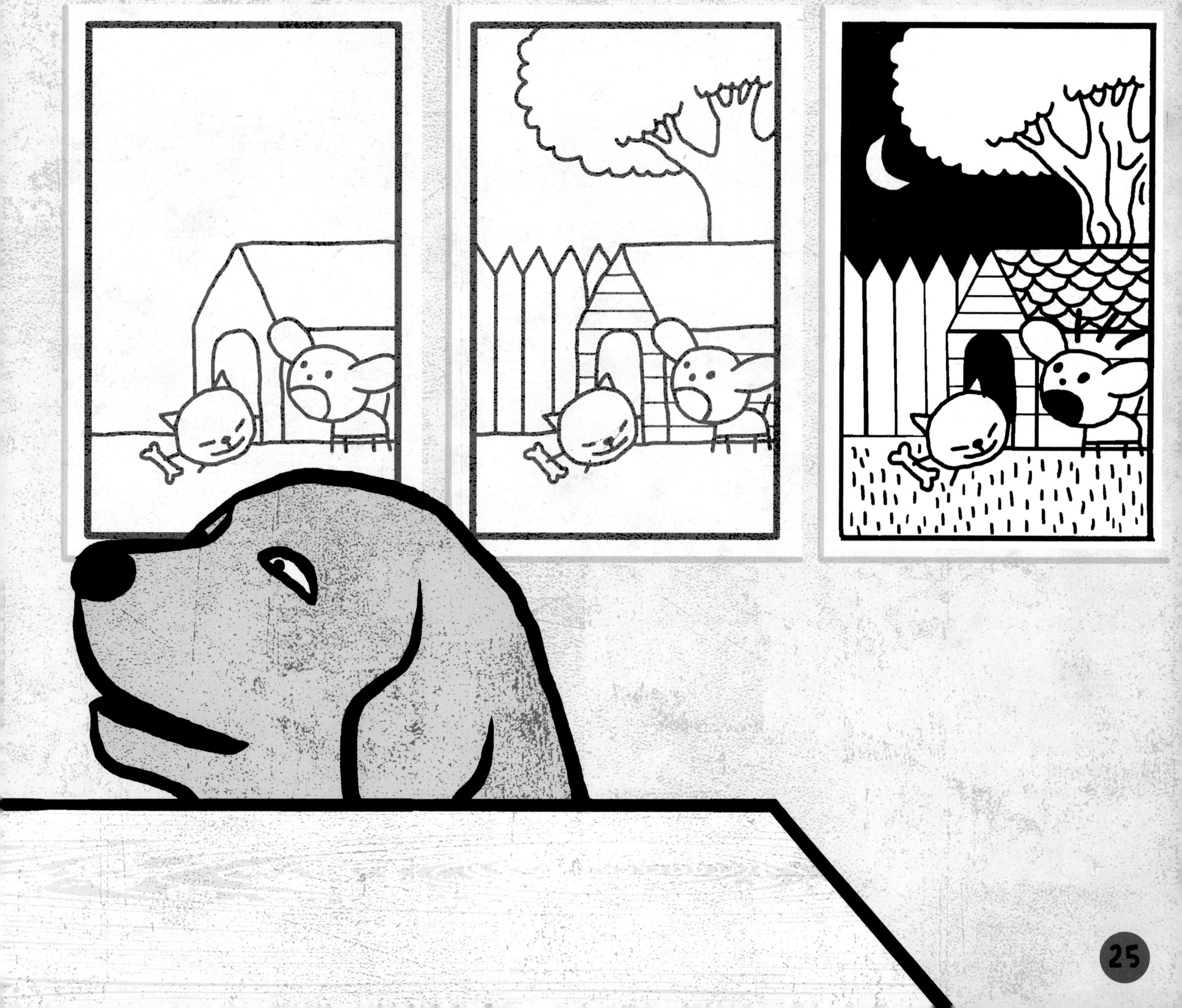

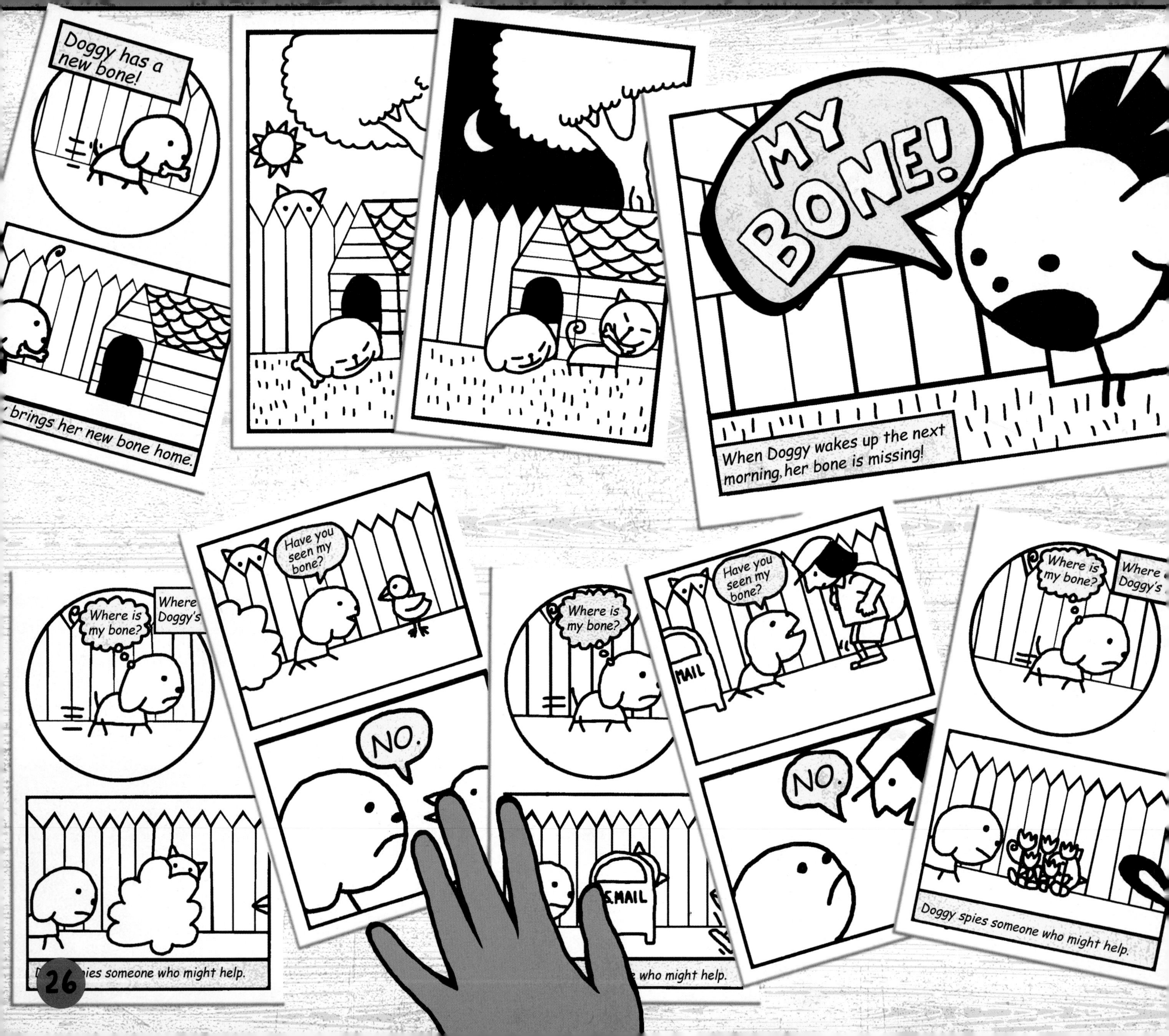

Doggy has a new bone!
brings her new bone home.
MY BONE!
When Doggy wakes up the next morning, her bone is missing!
Where is my bone?
Where Doggy's
ies someone who might help.
Have you seen my bone?
NO.
Where is my bone?
EMAIL
who might help.
Have you seen my bone?
MAIL
NO.
Where is my bone?
Where Doggy's
Doggy spies someone who might help.

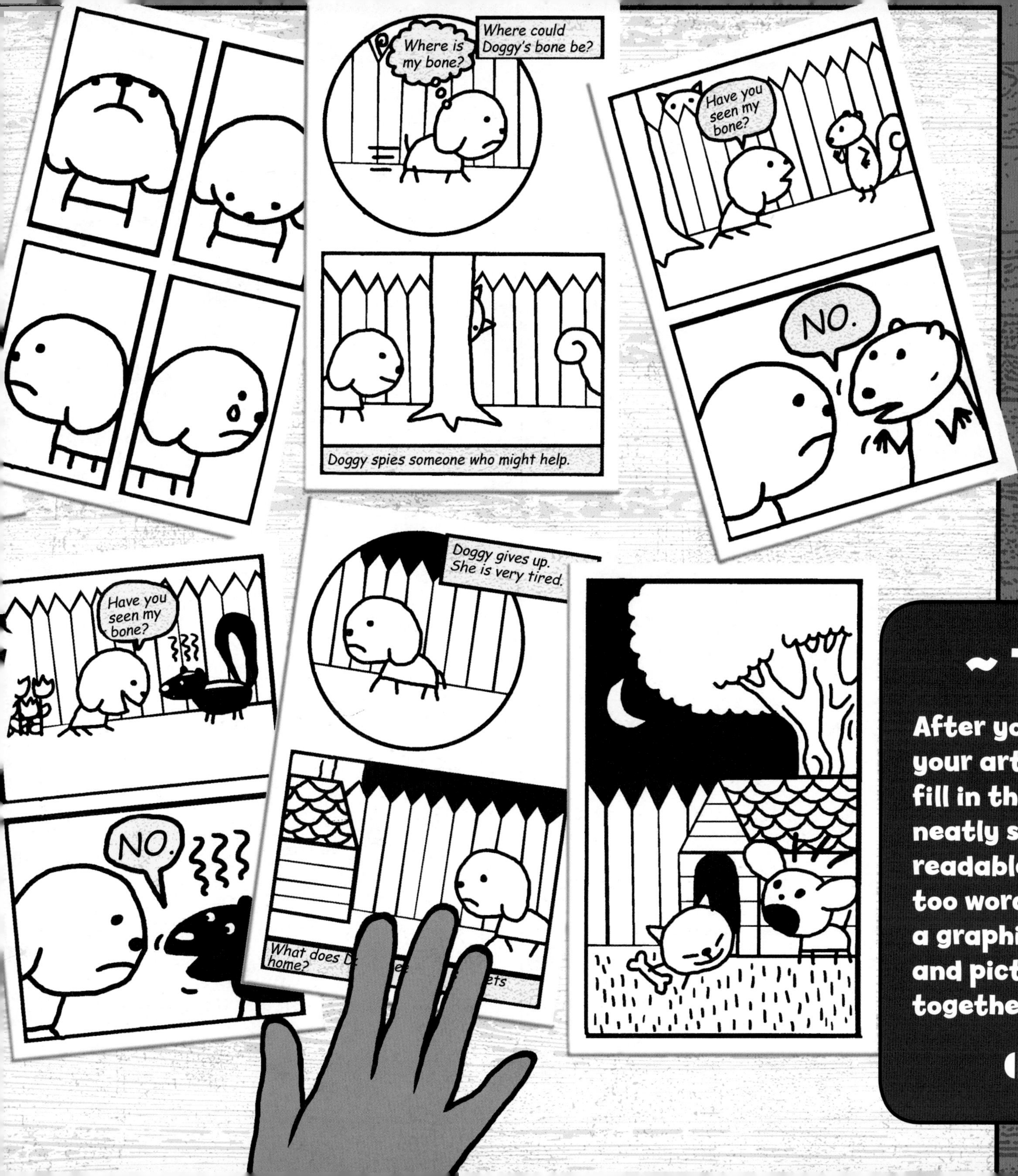

Where is my bone?
Where could Doggy's bone be?
Doggy spies someone who might help.
Have you seen my bone?
NO.
Have you seen my bone?
NO.
Doggy gives up. She is very tired.

~ Tool 11 ~

After you've finished your art, you'll need to fill in the WORDS. Print neatly so everything is readable. And don't get too wordy. Remember, in a graphic novel, the words and pictures should work together to tell the story.

Let's Review!

These are the **11 tools** you need to write great graphic novels.

To create a graphic novel, first RESEARCH **(1)** other graphic novels at a bookstore or library. BRAINSTORMING **(2)** will help you come up with story ideas. Once you have your CHARACTERS **(3)** figured out, give them a problem and write the PLOT **(4)**.

Next, draw THUMBNAIL SKETCHES **(5)** that focus on the action of the story. Deciding when to use pictures and words is very important. Create PANELS **(6)** to lay out your graphic novel. Using your thumbnail sketches as a guide, fill in the panels. Leave room for CAPTIONS and BUBBLES **(7)**. You might use EMANATA **(8)** to show the feelings of your characters. Sometimes, it's nice to break up your graphic novel with a SPLASH PAGE **(9)**. A BACKGROUND **(10)** can help bring the story to life. Finally, fill in the WORDS **(11)** of your story.

Getting Started Exercises

- Draw three panels of the same size. In the first panel, draw a person throwing a ball into the air. (Draw a stick figure if you want.) In the second panel, draw a dog jumping up and catching the ball. In the third panel, draw the dog running away with the ball. Congratulations! You've drawn an action sequence.

- Take the action sequence you drew in the first exercise, and add a background. Where are the person and dog? At a park? In the living room? Does the dog have a name? You may want to add speech bubbles or a caption. What is the dog thinking? Add thought bubbles!

- Turn a story you know into a graphic novel. Try *The Three Little Pigs*, for example. Draw thumbnail sketches to show how you would lay out the story. Focus on the story's action. Will you show each pig building his house? Or are the houses already built? Will you show the wolf walking up to the house? Will you use thought or speech bubbles? Captions? Can you capture the most exciting moment in a splash page?

Drawing Tips

 When you choose a main character for your graphic novel, know your drawing strengths. If you're a beginner, you may want to draw something simple, such as a stick figure. Or draw a more advanced figure. Remember, you'll draw the character over and over again!

 When drawing panels, use a ruler. You can make your panels the same size or change them.

 When there's an important or exciting moment in your story, you might want to use a splash page. Fill up the whole page with one big picture.

 Motion lines show movement. If a character is waving, draw curved lines around her hand. If a character is running, draw straight lines behind her.

Glossary

background—where the story takes place, the location

brainstorm—to come up with many ideas

caption—a box that contains words that go with a picture; also called a narrative box

character—a person, animal, or creature in a story

illustration—a piece of artwork that shows a scene from a story

narrative box—a box that contains words that go with a picture; also called a caption

panel—the building block of a graphic novel

plot—what happens in a story

research—reading and learning facts about a subject

sequence—one thing coming after another in a fixed order

setting—the time and place of a story

sketch—a quick, rough drawing

speech bubble—a rounded shape that contains a character's speech; also known as a speech balloon

splash page—a full-page illustration

thought bubble—a wavy shape that contains a character's thoughts; also known as a thought balloon

thumbnail sketch—a small, quick drawing

To Learn More

More Books to Read

Hayes, Geoffrey. *Benny and Penny in Just Pretend.* New York: RAW Junior, LLC, 2008.

Holm, Jennifer L., and Matthew Holm. *Babymouse: Dragonslayer.* Baby Mouse; 11. New York: Random House Children's Books, 2009.

Kinney, Jeff. *Diary of a Wimpy Kid: Greg Heffley's Journal.* New York: Amulet Books, 2007.

Reynolds, Aaron. *Tiger Moth, Insect Ninja.* Tiger Moth. Minneapolis: Stone Arch Books, 2007.

Internet Sites

FactHound offers a safe, fun way to find Internet sites related to this book. All of the sites on FactHound have been researched by our staff.

Here's all you do:
Visit *www.facthound.com*
FactHound will fetch the best sites for you!

Index

Look for all of the books in the Writer's Toolbox series:

Action! Writing Your Own Play
Art Panels, BAM! Speech Bubbles, POW! Writing Your Own Graphic Novel
It's All About You: Writing Your Own Journal
Just the Facts: Writing Your Own Research Report
Make Me Giggle: Writing Your Own Silly Story
Once Upon a Time: Writing Your Own Fairy Tale
Share a Scare: Writing Your Own Scary Story
Show Me a Story: Writing Your Own Picture Book
Sincerely Yours: Writing Your Own Letter
Words, Wit, and Wonder: Writing Your Own Poem